The Theology of Alcoholics Anonymous

A Guide to the Theological and Religious Underpinnings of AA

JACK S.

ISBN 979-8-88685-753-5 (paperback)
ISBN 979-8-88685-754-2 (digital)

Christian Faith Publishing
832 Park Avenue
Meadville, PA 16335
www.christianfaithpublishing.com

The author takes full responsibility for his understanding and interpretation of the AA program. No one person ever speaks for Alcoholics Anonymous.

Excerpts from AA materials are reprinted with permission of Alcoholics Anonymous World Services Inc. (AAWS). Permission to reprint these excerpts does not mean that AAWS has reviewed or approved the contents of this publication or that AA necessarily agrees with the views expressed herein. AA is a program of recovery from alcoholism only—use of the excerpts in connection with programs and activities that are patterned after AA, but which address other problems, or in any other non-AA context, does not imply otherwise.

Printed in the United States of America

CONTENTS

PREFACE

My name is Jack S., and I am an alcoholic. Over several years, I gradually became an alcoholic, transitioning from a heavy social drinker to a blackout drinker. During the last years of my drinking, I consumed a fifth of gin a day. I tried many times to stop drinking on my own, and occasionally, I could stop for periods of time (once for thirteen months). Inevitably, however, I would restart drinking and return to my previous levels of alcohol consumption.

In 1998, I found my way into Alcoholics Anonymous and was fortunate from the outset to have an excellent AA sponsor. Currently, I have been sober for twenty-three years and have never had a single drink during these years. For me, this has been a miracle for which I am forever grateful. There is little doubt that I would have been long dead from the effects of alcoholism had I not found my way into AA.

This book is *not* about my alcoholism story. Rather, it is an attempt to uncover and explain the underlying "theology" of AA and why the program works for so many people. Founded nearly ninety years ago by Bill Wilson and Dr. Bob Smith, AA has been successful in achieving long-term sobriety for hundreds of thousands of hardcore alcoholics. Why does AA—and sister programs like Narcotics Anonymous (NA)—work for many (though not all) alcoholics and addicts, and why is its underlying theology a key reason for AA's success? *That is the focus of this guide.*

I hold an MA degree in philosophy from Ohio State University and a Masters in Theological Studies (MTS) from Drew Theological School. I currently serve as a certified lay minister in the United Methodist Church.

There are three audiences for this book:

1. **The Unsober Alcoholic**

    Perhaps you've been worried about and struggling with your drinking. Perhaps there have already been some consequences from your drinking—e.g., divorce, DUI, loss of job, and so on. Maybe the title of this book about the "theology" of alcoholism intrigues you. Maybe you're an agnostic or an atheist who is put off by this title about the "theology" of AA. Please give this guide a chance. You might be surprised about this theology and why even the hard-core atheist can be a full and successful member of AA.

2. **Current AA Members**

    Perhaps you are already a member of AA and have some sober time but are interested in learning more about the disease of alcoholism, why AA works for so many people, and why the underlying theology is so critical to its success. Hopefully, this book will answer those questions and aid you in your journey of sobriety.

3. **Religious Leaders**

    Many religious leaders have recognized and supported AA for years. Churches and synagogues are often sites for AA meetings. However, many of these leaders do not fully understand why AA is so successful and what the religious and spiritual tenets of AA are. There is also much that these religious leaders can learn from the philosophy, theology, and operations of AA. Currently, there are over two million AA members in the U.S. alone, while many churches and synagogues have seen a decrease in membership over the past twenty years. Perhaps there are some key lessons for religious leaders in the following pages.

CHAPTER 1

The Disease of Alcoholism

Alcoholism is a chronic disease with a high mortality rate if untreated, with extremely high rates of health care and hospital costs and devastating effects on family life.

Problem drinking that becomes severe is now characterized by the medical community as "alcohol use disorder" or AUD. Severe AUD is a chronic relapsing brain disorder characterized by an *impaired ability to stop or control alcohol use despite adverse social, occupational, or health consequences.*[1] AUD is considered incurable but treatable. As the AA program repeatedly states, *"once an alcoholic, always an alcoholic,"*[2] but it is possible for the alcoholic to lead a completely sober life. AA literature is filled with stories of alcoholics who have maintained absolute sobriety for many years, who then relapsed and quickly resumed their previous levels of alcohol consumption. Once the alcoholic's brain has exhibited the physiological and biochemical characteristics of AUD, there is no return to their pre-AUD brain state.

Consider these devastating statistics:

- People ages 12 and older. According to the 2019 National Survey on Drug Use and Health (NSDUH[3]), 14.5 million (nearly 15 million) people ages 12 and older (5.3 percent of this age group) had AUD. This number includes 9.0 million men (6.8 percent of men in this age group) and 5.5 million women (3.9 percent of women in this age group).
- Youth ages 12 to 17. According to the 2019 NSDUH, an estimated 414,000 adolescents aged 12 to 17 (1.7 per-

cent of this age group) had AUD. This number includes 163,000 males (1.3 percent of males in this age group) and 251,000 females (2.1 percent of females in this age group).

- Excessive alcohol use is responsible for more than 95,000 deaths in the United States each year, or 261 deaths per day. These deaths shorten the lives of those who die by an average of almost 29 years, for a total of 2.8 million years of potential life lost. People hospitalized with alcohol use disorder have an average life expectancy of 47–53 years (men) and 50–58 years (women), and they die 24–28 years earlier than people in the general population.
- Alcohol overdoses alone caused 29,000 hospitalizations, and drug overdoses alone caused another 114,000. The cost of these hospitalizations now exceeds $1.2 billion per year just for people aged 18–24.
- The total cost of alcoholism includes the cost of drunk-driving accidents and the expense of curing related health problems. It has been estimated that alcoholism alone can cost up to $224 billion annually to society.
- Alcoholism within a family is a problem that can destroy a marriage or drive a wedge between members. That means alcoholic people can blow through the family budget, cause fights, ignore children, and otherwise impair the health and happiness of the people they love. One in five adult Americans have lived with an alcoholic relative while growing up. In general, these children are at greater risk for having emotional problems than children whose parents are not alcoholics.

Clearly, alcoholism (AUD) is a major disease affecting millions of people. It has a devasting impact on the alcoholic (alienating his or her family and friends, affecting job performance) and is driving up our nation's health-care costs exponentially. AA believes that it has a "solution" to this critical national problem.

CHAPTER 2

The Success of AA in treating Alcoholism

Alcoholic Anonymous, as an organization, takes no position on the efficacy of AA treatment. Many participants in AA would also support non-AA treatments if they were successful in treating an individual's alcoholism or addiction. AA and its participants make no claim that AA or NA (and other twelve-step programs) should be considered the *only* treatment method. AA is simply not for everyone for a variety of reasons.

However, evidence in the past two years indicates that AA or NA and similar twelve-step methods have the highest rate of achieving long-term (greater than one year) abstinence from alcoholism.

The charitable organization Cochrane[1] is a highly respected group of international researchers and health-care professionals who review and conduct health research projects. Here is a quick summary of their findings regarding AA and similar twelve-step programs:

> Manualized AA/TSF(Twelve Step Facilitation) interventions usually produced higher rates of continuous abstinence than the other established treatments investigated. Non-manualized AA/TSF performed as well as other established treatments.
>
> AA/TSF may be superior to other treatments for increasing the percentage of days of abstinence, particularly in the longer term. AA/TSF probably performs as well as other treatments for reducing

the intensity of drinking (of alcohol). AA/TSF probably performs as well as other treatments for alcohol-related consequences and addiction severity. Four of the five economics studies found substantial cost-saving benefits for AA/TSF, which indicate that AA/TSF interventions probably reduce health-care costs substantially. The evidence suggests that 42% of participants participating in AA would remain completely abstinent one year later, compared to 35% of participants receiving other treatments including CBT(Cognitive Behavior Therapy). This effect is achieved largely by fostering increased AA participation beyond the end of the TSF program.

What are the components of AA that account for its high rate of success? In the author's opinion, there are nine key reasons for its success:

1.   **Admission of Defeat**
     The successful participant in AA must admit, in the core of their being, that they are alcoholic and that they are unable (powerless) to control their drinking. In short, they must be willing to surrender to the program.

2.   **Willing to Go to Any Length**
     The participant must be willing to commit to following the methods and principles of AA. Halfhearted attempts will not work. Although initially, the participant may be "evaluating" the program for themselves, at some early stage, they must commit fully to the program. The AA participant must be willing to "take good orderly direction" from the program and their sponsor. AA is a total abstinence program. The participant must understand that they must commit to total abstinence and must understand that "the first drink will get you drunk."

3. **Ninety Meetings in Ninety Days**

   A test of that commitment is the willingness to attend and participate in daily AA meetings for ninety consecutive days. This immersion into the AA program helps the participant understand the program and adopt its methods for daily living. It is interesting that several clinical studies using PET scans indicate that the alcoholic's brain undergoes some modest improvements after ninety days of sobriety.[2]

4. **Reliance on a "Higher Power"**

   We will later discuss at some length the theology of AA and this notion of a "Higher Power." What is critical for AA participants is understanding that they are not their own higher power. They must accept that the individual cannot simply "will" to stop drinking but must rely on something or someone other than themselves to provide them with the strength or power to remain abstinent one day at a time.

5. **The Twelve Steps**

   The keystone of the AA and NA programs are the twelve steps. These were evolved from the six principles or tenets of the Oxford Groups[3] in the late 1930s. These six principles are as follows: a complete deflation, a dependence on God, a moral inventory, a confession, restitution, and continued work with others in need. Wilson and the early founders of AA divided and expanded these six principles into twelve steps (see appendix for the listing.) The AA "treatment plan" requires a rigorous adherence to these twelve steps. Taking the twelve steps of AA is only possible by continually practicing the virtues of honesty and humility. Although AA literature states that the twelve steps are only "suggestions," there appears to be a strong correlation between adherence to these twelve steps and long-term sobriety.

6. **The Fellowship**

   The participant in AA is urged to change "people, places, and things" if they want to be successful. This means that the participant is asked to change the environment or milieu of their drinking lives—that is, not to associate with drinking friends (at least initially), not to go to bars or parties where they drank (again, at least initially), and not to do the same things that they associated with their drinking lives. To help accomplish this major change, AA offers a variety of daily meetings where the participant can meet with other alcoholics and begin to establish new friendships and associations. Establishing a new network of friends in AA is vitally important. There are over two hundred thousand AA meetings daily in the U.S. 24/7, so there is no excuse for "not making a meeting." The mutual support that the participant finds in the AA fellowship is a critical success factor.

7. **The Use of an AA Sponsor**

   Early in the life of AA, the role of the "sponsor" became a key component of AA's success. Each AA participant is urged to have an AA sponsor who can help guide them in the program, especially in performing the twelve steps of AA. Today it has become vogue for all sorts of people to have mentors or coaches to assist them with various aspects of their personal and professional lives. AA was an early innovator of the sponsor (or mentor) concept, and it is a key component of its success.

8. **The Promise of Anonymity**

   Although the societal stigma of alcoholism has lessened in recent years, many newcomers to AA are concerned about people (especially employers) knowing that they are alcoholics. AA provides an ironclad promise of maintaining anonymity for all participants: "Leave the names and faces behind."

9. **The Unique Organizational Aspects of AA**
   There are several organizational aspects of AA that have helped ensure its long-term survival and has helped individual AA participants to maintain sobriety (see appendix for the Twelve Traditions and Twelve Concepts of AA). These aspects include the following:

- A clear and single focus—to help the person suffering from alcoholism achieve sobriety. That is the sole purpose of AA.
- No outside financial support and no positions on political or societal issues.
- No organizational hierarchy. There are support agencies and no ruling AA bodies other than the individual group meeting making decisions by a "group consciousness."
- No dues or fees required. There is no financial interest in AA, and funds are raised simply to support individual meetings.
- Sister programs, such as Al-Anon and Alateen, which provide education and support for family members and friends before and after the alcoholic comes into AA.

These nine components are key to the success of the AA treatment method. However, not everyone who believes that they have a "drinking problem" is able or willing to commit to the AA program and these principles. That is understandable, and these persons are urged to find another treatment program that, hopefully, will bring them relief from this deadly disease.

CHAPTER 3

AA Is a Spiritual Program

AA literature repeatedly states that it is a "spiritual" program that helps the participant have a "spiritual awakening" and helps achieve "spiritual progress."[1] AA claims that it is not a religious program, and many of its proponents do not belong to any religious organization, and they frequently espouse antireligious sentiments. Although AA was founded by "religious" people and was based on the tenets of a Christian renewal movement (namely, the Oxford Group), AA literature and participants claim that it is nonreligious in nature.

However, U.S. courts have repeatedly declared that AA is religious in nature and that courts cannot mandate anyone to participate in AA meetings.

"By 2001, two circuit courts, at least three district courts, and two state supreme courts had all considered whether prisoners or parolees could be forced to attend religion-based treatment programs. Their unanimous conclusion was that such coercion was unconstitutional."[2]

Since that time, additional courts agreed. For example, in 2007, a U.S. Circuit Court of Appeals heard *Inouye v. Kemna*. The court examined the AA program. It held that it had "such substantial religious components that governmentally compelled participation in it violated the Establishment Clause."

AA often argues that it is spiritual rather than religious. However, after carefully examining the evidence, the courts rejected that claim.

The courts have based their decisions on the following facts:

1. The twelve steps of AA frequently mention "God" and other religious concepts like prayer and meditation, and they are based on traditional religious concepts, like confession and repentance.
2. AA has regular meetings where these concepts are discussed, and participants are encouraged to follow these principles.

Certainly, AA is not like many other traditional religions, and calling it a "religion" is not warranted. Nevertheless, AA clearly has "religious aspects" and should be acknowledged as such by its participants.

Part of the confusion here is the failure to clearly define what we mean by "spiritual" and "religious."

The concept of *spirituality* is based on the metaphysical position that there is more to the universe and life than simply material and physical reality. There is a nonmaterial aspect to life and understanding, and connecting to this nonmaterial world is possible through various practices like prayer, various forms of meditation, and physical practices like yoga and Tai Chi. Spirituality is achieved through an individual's use of these various practices. Spirituality can be achieved separately from religion. AA views spiritual practice as a way of achieving "conscious contact with the God of one's understanding" and is meant to achieve a "spiritual awakening" in the AA participant, which leads to the transformation of the individual into a sober, sane, and productive human being.

The concept of *religion* is based on a belief system about the ultimate reality of the universe and the individual's ethical practices. Religion is always based on a group understanding and not simply individual understanding. Religions are organized and usually have some form of hierarchy to guide its practice and to make any changes in its belief system.

Here is a way of looking at this distinction between religion and spirituality. Note that these concepts overlap to some extent.

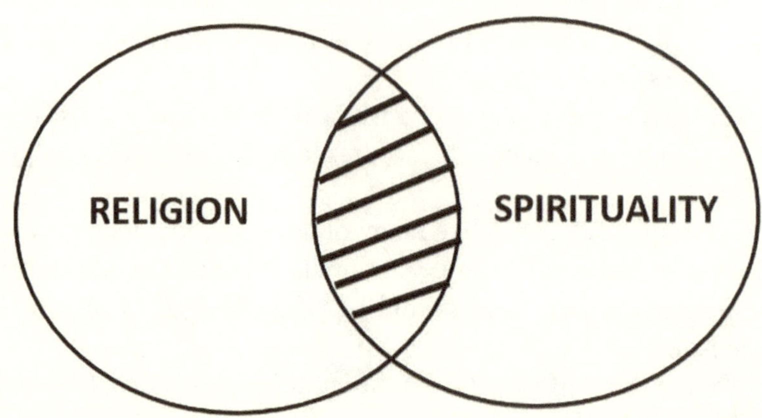

One can practice spirituality and be spiritual in nature without being a member of any religion. Likewise, some religions can assist their members in spiritual practices and growing more spiritual in nature. Some religious organizations, however, fail to achieve this goal. AA combines, to some extent, both concepts and should acknowledge that it is both religious and spiritual in nature.

CHAPTER 4

AA's Concept of God

Although AA literature is filled with references to "God," AA has no definition for this God. Instead, AA advocates that each member find his or her own understanding of God. All definitions are acceptable and can work in the AA program. The only requirement is that the "God of your understanding"[1] cannot be yourself. Whatever your "God" is must be external to the self.

This fluid and individual understanding of "God" has, no doubt, been the linchpin of AA's success. AA participants can have a traditional religious-based understanding of God (Christianity, Judaism, Islam, Hinduism, etc.), or they can opt for any external concept such as love, nature, spirit, universal force, or even nonspiritual understandings such as using the fellowship of AA as the individual's God. This acceptance of a variety of individual understandings of God has allowed AA to become a worldwide organization, and it allows even the agnostic or atheist to fully participate in the AA's program of recovery.

To the traditional religious person, this individualization of the meaning of God may seem heretical. However, one might be surprised by the variety of understandings and definitions of God of individual participants in any traditional religious organization. Many members would not adhere to the credal understanding of the God of their own faith. The fact is that all of us—as the theologian Paul Tillich declared—define "God" in our own way.

Whatever way an AA participant defines "God," there are two attributes about this God that are implicit in the AA program:

1. This AA God is providential. This God is immanent in the world and cares for and participates in helping guide nature, especially human beings. This God does not control all events but is able to help humans do the "will of God" by helping align the individual's will with the "will" of this providential God.
2. This AA God is powerful. This God is a "Higher Power" that the individual can "tap into" to relieve the compulsion of alcoholism and can assist the participant in growing "along spiritual lines."

It is noteworthy what traditional attributes of God are *not* implicit in the AA program:

- There is no notion that God must be eternal and outside time and space (i.e., transcendent).
- There is no notion that God must be responsible for the creation of the universe.
- There is no notion that this God must be omniscient, knowing all things past, present, and future.
- There is no notion that this God must be omnipotent. AA acknowledges that God must be powerful, but not necessarily all-powerful.
- There is no notion that God must be all-loving, all-merciful, all-just, and perfect. AA acknowledges the providential nature of "God," but it does not require or attribute these specific characteristics to God.

The religious participant in AA can certainly define their God with these traditional attributes if they so desire, but the nonreligious participant in AA is equally free to reject these attributes for the "God of their understanding."

It is interesting to note that many people today, both religious and nonreligious, have questions and problems with these traditional attributes for God. The most common problem, of course, is the problem of evil, especially nonhuman-caused evil such as disease and calamities. If one defines God as omnipotent, omniscient, perfect, and all-loving, why does this God allow evil to occur, especially to the innocent? This theodicy problem has been the bane of philosophers and theologians for centuries, and many people are skeptical about the proposed solutions to the theodicy question. AA escapes this problem by only positing two attributes to God: providence and power.

CHAPTER 5

AA's Concept of Grace

The most "religious" concept in the AA program of recovery is its concept of "grace." As previously stated, the AA "God" is both providential and powerful and can help transform the alcoholic's behavior and outlook on life. This transformation comes through the *offering and acceptance* of God's grace.

Traditionally and biblically, "grace" is defined as *a spontaneous gift from God to people*—"generous, free, and totally unexpected and undeserved"[1]—that takes the form of divine favor, love, clemency, and a share in the divine life of God. In AA, God's grace is a power or strength that allows alcoholics to do what they "previously could not do on their own." God offers this grace to all people even while they are "yet sinners." Even in the throes of his or her alcoholism, AA's God freely offers power, life, and strength to the raging alcoholic.

Grace has always been viewed as a two-way street, and this is certainly true in the AA program of recovery. Although we certainly do not earn God's grace by our good behavior (our works), AA believes that we must practice, or "take action," for God's grace to work in our lives. Traditionally, most religions have espoused certain "means of grace" for God's grace and power to be activated in our lives. These traditional means or practices of grace include regular worship attendance, prayer and meditation, reading of scripture or other religious texts, working with a spiritual director, participation in ceremonial rites (such as baptism, communion, confirmation), and charitable acts of mercy, including alms giving.

AA's means of grace, or "grace practices," include regular attendance at AA meetings, reading of AA literature, prayer and meditation, practicing the twelve steps, working with a sponsor, speaking commitments, sponsoring another alcoholic, attending and participating in AA celebrations, and performing works of charity, especially toward other suffering alcoholics.

The similarity between the traditionally religious means of grace and AA's means of grace is striking! There is a strong conviction among participants in AA that the regular and frequent practice of these means (actions) correlates with their strength to overcome the compulsion of alcoholism. These actions constitute the "acceptance" of God's grace and strength in our lives. Likewise, the failure to consistently take these actions, practice these means, will lead to "weakness" and, ultimately, relapse.

CHAPTER 6

The Role of Sin in AA

Both AA and the medical community have agreed for many years that alcoholism (AUD) is not a "moral failing." It is a result of physical and biochemical changes in the brain that cause the compulsive, destructive consumption of alcohol.

However, AA's position is somewhat enigmatic. The AA program infers that a cause of alcoholism is the alcoholic's allowance of "natural instincts" to become out of control, to "run wild." AA's position seems to be that the future alcoholic leads an "unmanageable" life focused on self-will and self-aggrandizement. The future alcoholic does not hold in check his or her naturally good instincts and leads a life of immorality and deceit. Simply put, the future alcoholic has an extensive list of character defects (or "sins") that are a *precedent* to AUD and actual brain physiological changes.

Furthermore, AA cautions its participants that, even when sober for several years, the alcoholic must continually work to control their instincts and lessen, if not eradicate, these "sinful" tendencies and actions. Unless the alcoholic continues to "be entirely ready to humbly ask God to remove these character defects (steps 6 and 7)," there is an increasing risk that the participant will relapse back to their previous alcoholic state.

AA's understanding of "character defect" is similar to the traditional meaning of sin (*hamartia*)—a "missing of the mark" (an ancient archery term). The "mark" is seen as the "will of God," and repeated misses, repeated failures to eliminate character defects result in weakening the alcoholic's resolve to remain sober. There is no implication that the bond between God and the alcoholic is severed by these defects. This differs from some traditional understandings of sin as a breaking in the relationship with God. AA does not appear to understand sin as breaking the God-human relationship.

CHAPTER 7

The Need for Confession

If anything, AA's position on the need for personal confession of one's character defects (sins) is stronger than most traditional religions. AA's steps 4 and 5 require AA participants to "make a thorough and fearless moral inventory of ourselves" and to "admit to God, to ourselves, and to another human being the exact nature of our wrongs." In fact, AA states these steps are so important that the failure to take them thoroughly will likely lead to a relapse.

These steps require extreme honesty and humility, especially since they are almost always made in personal meetings with the alcoholic's sponsor. Nothing is to be held back, and the participant is asked to specifically state their role and responsibility for each of these character defects. The focus of this inventory is often on the failures and consequent damage in the alcoholic's personal relationships.

AA's position is that unless there is a thorough "cleaning of the house," spiritual progress cannot be made, and one's sobriety and sanity is put at risk. It is noteworthy again that AA's requirement (suggestion?) here is more stringent than almost all religions', except for Roman and Orthodox Catholicism. Most Protestant denominations practice some form of "corporate confession" during their worship services but do not require personal confession to another human, such as a priest. Jews practice a form of confession and repentance primarily during the Day of Atonement—but again, not personally to a rabbi.

Perhaps we have substituted therapists, psychologists, and psychiatrists for our personal "confessors." There is, however, a significant difference between this "therapist confession" and AA's "sponsorship confession." During step 5, the sponsor will often share his or her own experience of character defects and moral failings with the sponsee. This almost never happens in a "therapist confession." This mutual sharing often lifts guilt from the participant and helps the participant learn forgiveness of others as they experience the forgiveness of step 5.

AA strongly emphasizes that the participant only takes their own inventory, to "clean only their side of the street." Like many religions, AA stresses the need for tolerance and forgiveness of others. Perhaps AA does a better job at this than many religious organizations.

CHAPTER 8

The Role of Repentance

Although AA does not use the term *repentance* in its literature, it is clear that "a turning around and away" from the alcoholic's previously sinful and unmanageable life is vital for spiritual awakening and progress. Simply confessing one's sins is not enough! The AA participant is directed in steps 6 and 7 to work on "repenting" from their previous life: "We became willing to ask God to help us remove our defects of character" and "humbly asked Him to remove our shortcomings." The AA program appreciates the fact that no one will ever fully eliminate all their character defects and sins. No one is perfect, but progress must be made.

Although the participant is urged to become willing and ready to work on all their character defects, there are two overarching character defects that inevitably must be improved upon:

1. **Resentments**

    Every alcoholic comes into AA usually with an extensive list of resentments. They feel they have been wronged by others and society and that their anger is perfectly "justified." They are often surprised to learn that AA teaches that "justified anger" is not acceptable for the alcoholic because he or she "cannot deal with it." The consumption of alcohol is used to soothe these feelings of resentment. The failure to eliminate resentments can trigger a relapse. The participant's sponsor often counsels two remedies for these resentments—namely, trying to focus on the participant's own role and responsibility for the situation and praying for the persons they believe are the cause of their resentment.

2. Unreasonable Fears

AA acknowledges that some fears are reasonable and justi-fied. Certainly, the participant's fear of relapsing is a good fear that can help prevent a relapse. But many alcoholic fears are unreasonable and can lead to a relapse. Often, alcohol has been used as an anesthetic to deaden both resentments and fears. Many people, especially alcohol-ics, tend to "awfulize" situations, fearing things and con-sequences that have little chance of occurring. Here the sponsor can help the participant rationally evaluate the situation. "Staying in the moment" and "living one day at a time" are AA mantras that can help the alcoholic (all people!) control, if not eliminate, their unreasonable fears.

CHAPTER 9

The Idea of Redemption

Continual spiritual progress—not perfection—is a key goal of the AA program because it is spiritual progress that enables the alcoholic to remain sober, sane, and become a productive member of society.

This notion of aiming toward perfection but understanding that only progress and not perfection is attainable, at least in this life, is a key concept in many religions. For example, John Wesley, the founder of Methodism, preached that grace draws us toward Christian perfection, which Wesley described as a heart "habitually filled with the love of God and neighbor" and as "having the mind of Christ and walking as he walked." For Wesley, this is how we "move on toward perfection."[1] This sentiment is consistent with AA's understanding of grace and spiritual progress, not spiritual perfection.

Although AA does not mention the word *redemption* or *salvation*, it is clear from the tenets of the program that redemption for the alcoholic is not simply sobriety but is a "psychic change" in the alcoholic's thinking and way of life. The AA participant becomes a new person who, guided by the will and grace of God, consistently wants to do "the next right thing." This AA understanding of redemption is like the Christian's understanding that "if anyone is in Christ, the new creation has come: The old has gone, the new is here."[2]

The AA program, if consistently followed, results not just in sobriety one day at a time but also in a radical transformation of the alcoholic person. Once transformed, the alcoholic almost always becomes more charitable and loving in their nature. This is why many AA participants would say that they would continue to go to AA meetings and continue to practice the twelve steps even if a "miracle cure" was found for alcoholism. As the AA saying goes, "We came for the drinking but stayed for the thinking."

Unlike some religions, AA understands redemption as a "transformation in this life," not as a reward in an "afterlife." AA takes no position on whether there is an afterlife or not.

CHAPTER 10

An Attitude of Gratitude

The AA program "promises" the participant (see appendix for the Twelve Promises of AA) that they will experience "a new freedom and happiness" if the participant is "painstaking about this phase of their development." This is a truth espoused by long-term AA members and is another reason they "keep coming."

The transformed participant adopts a new way of thinking, an "attitude of gratitude." From being a chronic complainer about life, the transformed alcoholic becomes increasingly grateful for even the smallest things in their lives.

This attitudinal adjustment in outlook is mirrored in many religious teachings. Consider the Psalmist's teaching:

> Bless the Lord, O my soul, and forget not all his
> benefits, who forgives all your iniquity, who heals
> all your diseases, who redeems your life from
> the pit, who crowns you with steadfast love and
> mercy, who satisfies you with good so that your
> youth is renewed like the eagle's.[3]

Anne Lamott, a renowned spiritual teacher and an alcoholic and addict, teaches that there are only two great prayers: "Help" and "Thank You." AA members would agree but emphasize that the second prayer is more important than the first.

CHAPTER 11

Lessons for Religious Leaders

Hopefully, this short guide on the theological underpinnings of the AA program will help religious leaders better understand how AA works and why it merits their continued support.

Here are some AA lessons for these leaders that may be applicable for improving the strategies and operations of their own religious organizations. These lessons include the following:

1. **Singleness of Purpose**

   Most participants first come into AA desperate for help. They have hit their bottom and are usually willing to go to any length to end the compulsion of drinking. AA has a single and clear definition of its mission or purpose: *Our primary purpose is to stay sober and help other alcoholics to achieve sobriety.* Every AA member knows this purpose and can recite it without hesitation.

   Compare this to most religious organizations. Most have written mission statements, and some have vision and value statements. These are all good and well, but ask the next five members of your religious organization what these statements say. You may be disappointed by their response! Religious organizations must not only have clear statements, they must get the buy-in and understanding of their memberships to be truly effective. You cannot over-communicate your purpose or mission to your members.

2. **Acceptance of All**

One of the most remarkable aspects of AA is that *all* persons are welcome, accepted, and fully equal in AA. It does not matter what gender, what religion or nonreligion, what race or ethnicity, what nationality, what sexual orientation, what social status, or what education the participant has. They are fully accepted as equals in AA. In fact, people are often surprised to learn that people in the ravages of the disease, who are falling down drunk, are fully welcome at AA meetings provided they do not disrupt the meeting with their behavior. The only requirement for membership is *a desire to stop drinking*. Even when an AA participant relapses, they are fully welcomed back in the fellowship.

Again, compare this with some religious organizations. Some religious organizations are de facto segregated and have restrictions on the roles of women and LGBTQI persons in their organizations and belief systems. Even the most progressive religious organizations have a long way to go to match the true equality of AA. Perhaps this is one reason why so many of these organizations are losing members, especially millennials and young people.

3. **Spirituality Training**

AA constantly stresses for its members the need for spiritual practices and spiritual progress. Daily meditation and prayer are emphasized, and the AA program has several set prayers for the members to use frequently: The Serenity Prayer, The Lord's Prayer, the Prayer of St. Francis, and the Third-Step and Seventh-Step Prayers, to name a few. Daily spiritual reading is also stressed, such as AA's *Daily Reflections*. Matt Talbot spiritual retreats are conducted frequently for AA members.

In fairness, most religious organizations also teach and stress spiritual practices. But look at the members' attendance at Bible studies, prayer meetings, religious retreats, and small groups. Usually, the attendance at these offerings is a small percentage of the overall membership. Simple attendance at weekly worship services is not sufficient for spiritual and discipleship development. In fact, the average member is now only attending two worship services a month! We should not be surprised then when they "feel" that membership is not meeting their needs. The problem is age-old: "You can lead a horse to the water, but you can't make them drink it."

4. **Flattening the Hierarchy**

AA has a very flat organizational structure. There are no AA officers, no dictates from above, no fees paid to national. There are AA service organizations that provide materials and books to local meetings and communicate about statewide and international meetings. In essence, there is no hierarchy in AA.

Again, compare this to many mainline religious organizations. Many local churches and other religious organizations are required to financially support their hierarchies. Many members ask if they are getting value for their money. As local finances get tighter and tighter due to loss of membership, resentment grows, which can fuel a further loss in membership. To survive, all religious organizations must flatten their organizational structures.

Conclusion

If there are such things as miracles, then the founding of AA and its subsequent history of nearly ninety years certainly qualifies as one. In 1933, Bill Wilson was hospitalized four times for his acute alcoholism. He was considered a hopeless case. In 1934, he was visited in his Brooklyn apartment by an old drinking buddy, Ebby Thatcher, who was sober and a member of the Oxford Groups. Ebby encouraged Bill to "get religion." Wilson told him he couldn't accept any of that religious God stuff. Ebby told him to find the "God of his own understanding."

On December 11, 1934, Wilson was admitted for the final time to Townes Hospital in New York City. While there, he had a profound spiritual experience—a "white light" experience like those described by William James in his monumental work, *Varieties of Religious Experience*. The compulsion to drink was lifted from Wilson, and he never had another drink till his death in 1971.

In 1935, Wilson, while visiting Akron, Ohio, on a business trip, met another suffering alcoholic, Dr. Bob Smith. Their meeting and first discussion are considered the starting date of AA. Since that time, AA has expanded into more than two hundred countries and is successfully treating thousands upon thousands of alcoholics worldwide. If that's not a miracle, then what is?

ACKNOWLEDGMENTS

Although I take full responsibility for my interpretation of the AA program and its theological foundation, I could not have written this manuscript without the review and suggestions of several AA sisters and brothers and several religious persons who took the time to carefully read and suggest changes to the manuscript.

In particular, I thank my sponsor, Bob B. With forty-three years of sobriety, he has been a guiding influence and a supportive friend in my life. I also thank my other AA colleagues—Pete S., Lew K., John F., Mary D., Marc C., Rick R., and Herb K.—who reviewed and made important recommendations to improve the manuscript.

I also acknowledge the review and suggestions of Rev. Luana Cook Scott, Rev. Gabriel Corbett, Rev. Kris Hansen, and Bishop William Boyd Grove for their unfailing support for my AA journey.

Finally, I thank and acknowledge my wonderful wife Mary Ann, my son Christopher, and my daughter Lisa, who have been with me all the way on this journey and who made many helpful recommendations to improve this manuscript.

APPENDICES

THE TWELVE STEPS OF AA

AA's twelve-step approach follows a set of guidelines designed as "steps" toward recovery, and members can revisit these steps at any time. The Twelve Steps[9] are as follows:

1. We admitted we were powerless over alcohol—that our lives had become unmanageable.
2. Came to believe that a Power greater than ourselves could restore us to sanity.
3. Made a decision to turn our will and our lives over to the care of God as we understood Him.
4. Made a searching and fearless moral inventory of ourselves.
5. Admitted to God, to ourselves, and to another human being the exact nature of our wrongs.
6. Were entirely ready to have God remove all these defects of character.
7. Humbly asked Him to remove our shortcomings.
8. Made a list of all persons we had harmed, and became willing to make amends to them all.
9. Made direct amends to such people wherever possible, except when to do so would injure them or others.
10. Continued to take personal inventory and, when we were wrong, promptly admitted it.
11. Sought through prayer and meditation to improve our conscious contact with God as we understood Him, praying only for knowledge of His will for us and the power to carry that out.

12. Having had a spiritual awakening as the result of these steps, we tried to carry this message to alcoholics and to practice these principles in all our affairs.

THE TWELVE TRADITIONS OF AA

1. Our common welfare should come first; personal recovery depends upon AA unity.

2. For our group purpose, there is but one ultimate authority—a loving God as He may express Himself in our group conscience. Our leaders are but trusted servants; they do not govern.

3. The only requirement for AA membership is a desire to stop drinking.

4. Each group should be autonomous except in matters affecting other groups or AA as a whole.

5. Each group has but one primary purpose—to carry its message to the alcoholic who still suffers.

6. An AA group ought never endorse, finance, or lend the AA name to any related facility or outside enterprise lest problems of money, property, and prestige divert us from our primary purpose.

7. Every AA group ought to be fully self-supporting, declining outside contributions.

8. Alcoholics Anonymous should remain forever nonprofessional, but our service centers may employ special workers.

9. AA, as such, ought never be organized; but we may create service boards or committees directly responsible to those they serve.

10. Alcoholics Anonymous has no opinion on outside issues; hence, the AA name ought never be drawn into public controversy.
11. Our public relations policy is based on attraction rather than promotion; we need always maintain personal anonymity at the level of press, radio, and films.
12. Anonymity is the spiritual foundation of all our traditions, ever reminding us to place principles before personalities.

THE TWELVE CONCEPTS OF AA

1. The final responsibility and the ultimate authority for AA world services should always reside in the collective conscience of our whole fellowship.

2. When, in 1955, the AA groups confirmed the permanent charter for their General Service Conference, they thereby delegated to the Conference complete authority for the active maintenance of our world services and thereby made the Conference—excepting for any change in the Twelve Traditions or in Article 12 of the Conference Charter—the actual voice and the effective conscience for our whole Society.

3. As a traditional means of creating and maintaining a clearly defined working relation between the groups, the Conference, the AA General Service Board, and its several service corporations, staffs, committees and executives, and of thus ensuring their effective leadership, it is here suggested that we endow each of these elements of world service with a traditional "Right of Decision."

4. Throughout our Conference structure, we ought to maintain at all responsible levels a traditional "Right of Participation," taking care that each classification or group of our world servants shall be allowed a voting representation in reasonable proportion to the responsibility that each must discharge.

5. Throughout our world service structure, a traditional "Right of Appeal" ought to prevail, thus assuring us that minority opinion will be heard and that petitions for the redress of personal grievances will be carefully considered.

6. On behalf of AA as a whole, our General Service Conference has the principal responsibility for the maintenance of our world services, and it traditionally has the final decision respecting large matters of general policy and finance. But the Conference also recognizes that the chief initiative and the active responsibility in most of these matters should be exercised primarily by the trustee members of the Conference when they act among themselves as the General Service Board of Alcoholics Anonymous.

7. The Conference recognizes that the Charter and the Bylaws of the General Service Board are legal instruments: that the trustees are thereby fully empowered to manage and conduct all the world service affairs of Alcoholics Anonymous. It is further understood that the Conference Charter itself is not a legal document: that it relies instead upon the force of tradition and the power of the AA purse for its final effectiveness.

8. The trustees of the General Service Board act in two primary capacities:
    a. With respect to the larger matters of overall policy and finance, they are the principal planners and administrators. They and their primary committees directly manage these affairs.
    b. But with respect to our separately incorporated and constantly active services, the relation of the trustees is mainly that of full stock ownership and of custodial oversight, which they exercise through their ability to elect all directors of these entities.

9. Good service leaders, together with sound and appropriate methods of choosing them, are at all levels indispensable for our future functioning and safety. The primary world service leadership once exercised by the founders of AA

must necessarily be assumed by the trustees of the General Service Board of Alcoholics Anonymous.

10. Every service responsibility should be matched by an equal service authority—the scope of such authority to be always well defined whether by tradition, by resolution, by specific job description, or by appropriate charters and bylaws.

11. While the trustees hold final responsibility for AA's world service administration, they should always have the assistance of the best possible standing committees, corporate service directors, executives, staffs, and consultants. Therefore, the composition of these underlying committees and service boards, the personal qualifications of their members, the manner of their induction into service, the systems of their rotation, the way in which they are related to each other, the special rights and duties of our executives, staffs, and consultants, together with a proper basis for the financial compensation of these special workers, will always be matters for serious care and concern.

12. The Conference shall observe the spirt of AA tradition, taking care that it never becomes the seat of perilous wealth of power; that sufficient operating funds and reserve be its prudent financial principle; that it places none of its members in a position of unqualified authority over others; that it reaches all important decisions by discussion, vote, and whenever possible, substantial unanimity; that its actions never be personally punitive nor an incitement to public controversy; that it never performs acts of government; that, like the Society it serves, it will always remain democratic in thought and action.

THE TWELVE PROMISES OF AA

If we are painstaking about this phase of our development, we will be amazed before we are halfway through. We are going to know a new freedom and a new happiness. We will not regret the past or wish to shut the door on it. We will comprehend the word *serenity*, and we will know peace. No matter how far down the scale we have gone, we will see how our experience can benefit others. That feeling of uselessness and self-pity will disappear. We will lose interest in selfish things and gain interest in our fellows. Self-seeking will slip away. Our whole attitude and outlook upon life will change. Fear of people and of economic insecurity will leave us. We will intuitively know how to handle situations that used to baffle us. We will suddenly realize that God is doing for us what we could not do for ourselves.

Are these extravagant promises? We think not. They are being fulfilled among us—sometimes quickly, sometimes slowly. They will always materialize if we work for them.

NOTES

Chapter 1

1. National Institute on Alcohol Abuse and Alcoholism: Understanding Alcohol Use Disorder.
2. *Alcoholics Anonymous Big Book,* p. 33.
3. National Survey on Drug Use and Health: Data Survey, p. 35 and following.

Chapter 2

1. The Cochrane Database of Systematic Reviews (CDSR) is the leading journal and database for systematic reviews in health care. CDSR includes Cochrane Reviews (systematic reviews) and protocols for Cochrane Reviews, as well as editorials and supplements.
2. ScienceDaily: "PET/CT reveals adaptations of the alcoholic brain" Study shows how the sober brain might protect against further relapse by limiting receptor activity linked to cravings (June 13, 2016).
3. The Oxford Group was a Christian organization (first known as First Century Christian Fellowship) founded by the American Lutheran Christian priest Frank Buchman in 1921. Buchman believed that the root of all problems were the personal problems of fear and selfishness. Further, Buchman believed that the solution to living with fear and selfishness was to "surrender one's life over to God's plan." (Wikipedia)

Chapter 3

1. *Alcoholics Anonymous Big Book,* p. 60.
2. The Second Circuit Court decision states that AA "placed a heavy emphasis on spirituality and prayer, in both conception and in practice," that participants were told to "pray to God," and that meetings began and adjourned with "group prayer." The court therefore had "no doubt" that AA meetings were "intensely religious."

Chapter 4

1. *Alcoholics Anonymous Big Book,* p. 59.

Chapter 5

1. In Western Christian theology, grace is the help given to us by God because God desires us to have it, not necessarily because of anything we have done to earn it. It is understood by Christians to be a spontaneous gift from God to people—"generous, free, and totally unexpected and undeserved"—that takes the form of divine favor, love, clemency, and a share in the divine life of God. (Wikipedia)

Chapter 9

1. John Wesley, *A Plain Account of Christian Perfection.*
2. 2 Corinthians 5:17.
3 Psalm 147.

ABOUT THE AUTHOR

Jack S. is a Christian and currently serves as a certified lay minister in the Morristown United Methodist Church in Morristown, New Jersey. He holds a master's degree in theological studies from Drew University in Madison, New Jersey, and a master's degree in philosophy from the Ohio State University. Jack has been sober for twenty-three years due to the miracle of the Alcoholics Anonymous (AA) program, which he regularly attends and follows. His professional career was in health-care administration, serving as Vice President for Quality Management for a major health-care system. He is now retired and lives in Morris Plains, New Jersey, with his wife. He is blessed with two children and five grandchildren.

www.ingramcontent.com/pod-product-compliance
Lightning Source LLC
Chambersburg PA
CBHW031002180726
47993CB00018B/1521